Pass Functional Skills

Functional Skills Maths Level 2 Mini Tests

Revise and Practice for your Functional Skills Maths Level 2 Exam

Kieran Stinson

Copyright © 2022 Pass Functional Skills

All rights reserved.

ISBN: 9798797355540

Functional Skills Maths Level 2 Course

You are unique...

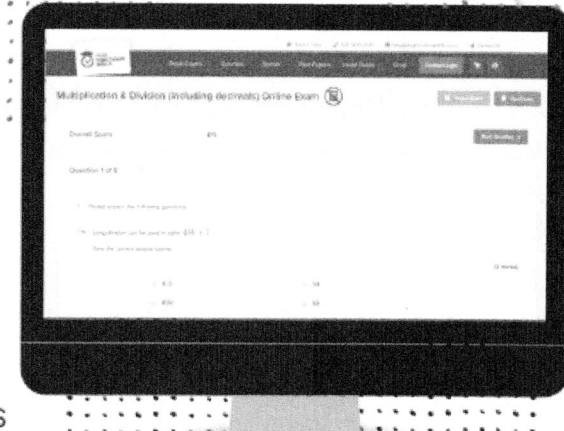

- ✓ Virtual **exam mocks**
- ✓ **Personalised** topic recommendations
- ✓ Detailed **video explanations**
- ✓ **100's** of practice questions
- ✓ Learn on **your own** schedule
- ✓ **Expertly designed** course

Shouldn't your **learning** be too?

Get learning at pfs.la/courses

About these tests

These tests have been written by a Functional Skills Maths expert, with the help of mathematicians, tutors, and expert teachers, to create 20 mini exams with a detailed mark scheme, showing you how your exam would be marked.

Once you have revised all the content, these short tests are the best way to assess your current ability and help you prepare for your exam. All the questions are relevant to every major exam board, including AQA, Edexcel, City & Guilds, NCFE, Open Awards and Highfield Qualifications.

The total amount of marks for each test is 10 marks, therefore it is advised that the maximum amount of time you spend on each test is 20 minutes, which will match up with the time constraints in a real exam (approximately 2 minutes per mark).

Tests that do not allow you to use a calculator will have this symbol next to the test number:

All tests without this symbol allow you to use a calculator, however this doesn't mean that you will necessarily need a calculator for all the questions in these tests.

Advice

For questions worth more than 1 mark, you will often receive marks for showing correct working or an attempt at using the correct method. Therefore, make sure to write down all your working, as this will help maximize your marks in preparation for your exam.

Furthermore, when checking your answers, use your common sense to see whether your answer seems appropriate using the context of the question. If you have time, you may find it useful to repeat key calculations in questions to check it is correct.

Make sure to read each question thoroughly and take note of the degree of accuracy you should give your answer to e.g., "Give your answer to 1 decimal place". If the question doesn't state this, usually giving your answers to 1 or 2 decimal places is acceptable.

Finally, always add units to answers where appropriate, as often you may lose a mark for not putting the correct unit in.

Functional Skills Maths Level 2
Revision Fundamentals

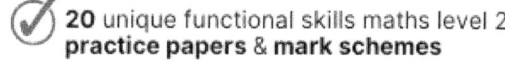

- ✓ **20** unique functional skills maths level 2 **practice papers** & **mark schemes**
- ✓ **Recommended** by **tutors** and **colleges**
- ✓ **Designed** by **experts**

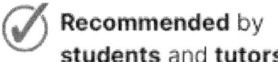

- ✓ **Recommended** by **students** and **tutors**
- ✓ Relevant to **all exam boards**
- ✓ Covers **all topics** in your exam

- ✓ Papers from the **exam board** of your choice
- ✓ **Explanations, practice questions** and **exam questions** on every topic
- ✓ **Save** with the bundle **discount**

Fill your boots...
...with essential **revision supplies**!

Get prepared at pfs.la/shop

Functional Skills Maths Level 2
Exam and Course

WHAT DO I GET?

- **Online** Exam
- **Hundreds** of practice questions
- Get into **Uni**, **Nursing**, **Policing**, **Apprenticeships**...

Take your **exam** from  **home!**

FREE RESIT with every **Exam + Online Course** purchase

- Unique **progress tracking**
- **39** comprehensive **topic sections**
- **Video Tutorials** and full **Mock Exams**

Get started at pfs.la/shop

Contents

Using Numbers 6
   Test 1 6
   Test 2 9
   Test 3 12
   Test 4 14
   Test 5 17
   Test 6 20
   Test 7 23
   Test 8 26
Common Measures, Shape, and Space 29
   Test 9 30
   Test 10..33
   Test 11..36
   Test 12..40
   Test 13..43
   Test 14..47
   Test 15..49
   Test 16..52
Handling Information and Data.. 56
   Test 17..57
   Test 18..60
   Test 19..63
   Test 20..67
Answers 71
   Using Numbers 71
   Common Measures, Shape and Space 76
   Handling Information and Data 81

Using Numbers

 **Test 1**

Q1

Order the following numbers from smallest to largest:

$$-2.071, \quad 0.2071, \quad 2.017, \quad -2.701, \quad -2.710$$

[1 mark]

Q2

Calculate the following:

$$68.52 - 11.673$$

[1 mark]

Q3

Calculate the following:

$$\frac{13}{6} - \frac{7}{4}$$

Give your answer in its simplest form.

[2 marks]

Q4

Estimate

$$\frac{12.31 \times 1.92}{4.86 + 3.07}$$

[1 mark]

Q5

Calculate the following:

$$211 \times 42$$

[2 marks]

Q6

Erin is making some chocolate cupcakes.

Part of the recipe includes cocoa powder, self-raising flour, and unsalted butter, which needs to be in the ratio $2 : 6 : 9$.

If 40 g of cocoa powder makes 12 cupcakes, how much self-raising flour does Erin need to make 24 cupcakes?

[3 marks]

Working space:

 **Test 2**

Q1

Order the following fractions from smallest to largest:

$$\frac{4}{9} \quad \frac{5}{12} \quad \frac{1}{3} \quad \frac{3}{4}$$

[2 marks]

Q2

Calculate

$$3 \times 6 + 3 - (8 \div 2)$$

[1 mark]

Q3

Write $\frac{7}{20}$ as a percentage.

[1 mark]

Q4

Given that $a = 4$ and $b = -1$

Find the value of $3ab + 5a^2$

[1 mark]

Q5

A group of 10 friends go on a camping trip and work out they have brought enough food to last them 12 days.

After 4 days, 2 members of the group decide to go home.

How many days would the remaining food last the rest of the group, assuming the rate of consumption per person remained the same?

[3 marks]

Q6

Hannah receives £50 from her grandparents; she decides to buy a top with the money.

She now has $\frac{7}{10}$ of the amount she received from her grandparents.

Calculate the amount that she paid for the top.

[2 marks]

Working space:

 **Test 3**

Q1

Calculate 30% of £84.

[2 marks]

Q2

In the number 12.438, what is the value of the digit 3?

[1 mark]

Q3

In the boxing day sales, a TV's price was reduced by 15%.

If the original price was £420, what is its price after the reduction?

[2 marks]

Q4

Alice and Brandon split £70 in the ratio 9 : 5.

Alice then spends 40% of her share on a pair of jeans, whereas Brandon spends 60% of his share on a pair of shoes.

Express the amount of money that Alice and Brandon spent, as a ratio in its simplest form.

[4 marks]

Q5

Calculate the following:

$$112.29 + 8.46$$

[1 mark]

Working space:

 **Test 4**

Q1

Tim's car shows that it has enough fuel in it to go 150 miles.

Tim then puts some fuel in his car, and now it shows it has 240 miles worth of fuel left.

Calculate the percentage increase in the distance the car will be able to travel with the current fuel level.

[2 marks]

Q2

Write 0.15 as a fraction in its simplest form.

[1 mark]

Q3

Leo gets paid £9.87 per hour on weekdays and £12.34 per hour on weekends.

Last week he worked 28 hours from Monday to Friday and then 6 hours on Sunday.

Estimate how much Leo got paid last week.

[3 marks]

Q4

Calculate the following:

$$188 \div 8$$

[1 mark]

Q5

It took 3 people 10 days to put up a fence around a garden.

If everyone worked at the same rate, how long would it have taken 5 people to put up the fence?

[3 marks]

Working space:

Test 5

Q1

Find the value of p, when $q = 3$, $r = -2$ and $s = 5$

Given that

$$p = \frac{r^2 - 8s}{3q}$$

[1 mark]

Q2

Calculate the following:

$$(12 + 9 \div 3) \times 4$$

[1 mark]

Q3

Eleanor and Carrie both put some of their monthly income into two separate savings accounts.

Eleanor saves 30% of her monthly income and Carrie saves $\frac{1}{4}$ of her monthly income.

After 3 months Eleanor and Carrie have £1890 and £1650 in their respective savings accounts.

If they earn no interest from the savings accounts, who has the greater monthly income?

[3 marks]

Q4

Calculate the following:

$$\frac{2}{9} + \frac{3}{5}$$

Give your answer in its simplest form.

[2 marks]

Q5

Change the following number from words to numbers:

One million, four hundred and thirty thousand, two hundred and eight

[1 mark]

Q6

Ruth is given $\frac{3}{8}$ of £60.

Gwen is given $\frac{4}{7}$ of £42.

Calculate who is given the most money.

[2 marks]

Working space:

Test 6

Q1

At the end of the month a car salesman offers a 15% discount on a car to try and make one final sale for the month.

The price of the car after the discount is £4760.

What was the original price of the car?

[2 marks]

Q2

What is the value of the digit 2 in 4621.53?

[1 mark]

Q3

Martin is making pancakes, using the following ingredients:

100 g of plain flour

2 large eggs

300 ml of milk

This recipe makes 8 pancakes.

Work out how much of each ingredient Martin would need to make 20 pancakes.

[3 marks]

Q4

What is $\frac{7}{40}$ as a percentage?

[1 mark]

Q5

A shop keeper wants to buy 1600 chocolate bars for her shop.

A box contains 25 packets of chocolate bars, with each packet containing 12 chocolate bars.

How many boxes will the shop keeper need to buy to have his desired amount of chocolate bars?

[3 marks]

Working space:

Test 7

Q1

Calculate the following

$$\frac{6}{13} + \frac{7}{8}$$

Give your answer in its simplest form.

[2 marks]

Q2

A laptop price decreased from £499 to £449 in a sale.

Calculate the percentage decrease, giving your answer to 2 decimal places.

[2 marks]

Q3

The formula for the volume of sphere is:

$V = \frac{4}{3}\pi r^3$, where r is the radius of the sphere.

Using this formula, calculate the volume of a sphere with a radius of 3.8 cm, stating the units.

Give your answer to 2 decimal places.

Use $\pi = 3.14$.

[3 marks]

Q4

Order the following numbers from largest to smallest.

0.00301,   0.01033,   0.01303,   0.10031,   0.01313

[1 mark]

Q5

Nathan, Isabella, and Tanya are three siblings with a combined age of 51.

The ratio of their ages is 4 : 5 : 8.

How old is each sibling?

[2 marks]

Working space:

Test 8

Q1

Mikayla hires two bikes for 6 hours for herself and her daughter from a company that offers bike rentals in a country park. To hire a bike there is an upfront cost of £5 plus £3.50 per hour. It is mandatory to wear a helmet, which cost £2.50 each to hire.

Calculate the total amount Mikayla spent.

[2 marks]

Q2

Calculate the following:

$$2\frac{2}{7} - 1\frac{3}{4}$$

[2 marks]

Q3

Lauren is looking at buying a tablet which has a RRP (recommended retail price) of £249.

Tech Essentials have an offer of $\frac{1}{8}$ off all tablets.

Digital Age also have an offer of 15% off all products.

Calculate which shop offers the best discount and state the sale price at this shop.

[2 marks]

Q4

A local council are turning an area of wasteland into a sports field.

An area with a size of 30000 m² has been marked out to turf.

Initially, the council hires 6 people to prepare the ground and lay the new turf.

After 8 days, the workers have turfed 12000 m² of the field.

The council want the sports field to be ready in time for the summer holidays, which means that the maximum total time to finish the sports field would be 10 days.

Work out the number of additional workers the council needs to hire for the remaining final 2 days to ensure that the sports field is ready in time for the summer holidays.

[4 marks]

Working space:

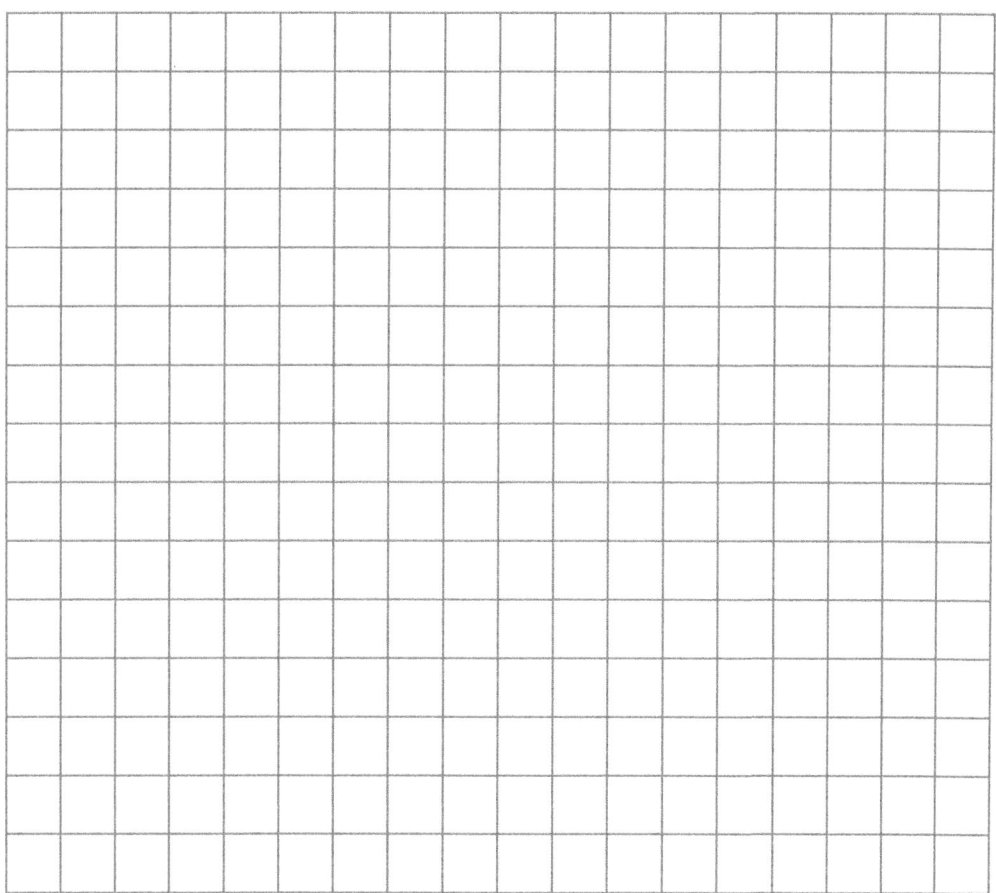

Functional Skills Maths Level 2 Course

You are unique...

- ✓ Virtual **exam mocks**
- ✓ **Personalised** topic recommendations
- ✓ Detailed **video explanations**
- ✓ **100's** of practice questions
- ✓ Learn on **your own** schedule
- ✓ **Expertly designed** course

Shouldn't your *learning* be too?

Get learning at pfs.la/courses

Common Measures, Shape, and Space

Test 9

Q1

Sophia is on holiday in Florida.

She visits a water park and buys a day pass for $134.

Calculate how much the day pass cost in pounds (£), given that £1 = $1.30.

[2 marks]

Q2

Find the perimeter of the rectangle below:

11.2 cm

Not drawn to scale

7.45 cm

[2 marks]

Q3

The diagram below shows the right-angled isosceles triangle ABC inside a circle, where $AC = CB$.

The circle has a diameter of 8.5 cm, and point C of the triangle is also the centre of the circle.

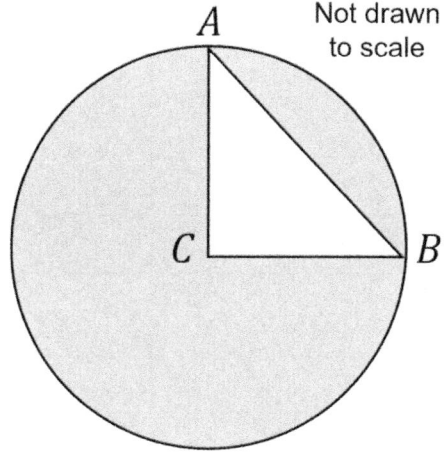

Not drawn to scale

Find the area of the shaded section of the diagram.

Use $\pi = 3.14$

[4 marks]

Q4

The diagram below shows an isosceles triangle.

Find the angle, x.

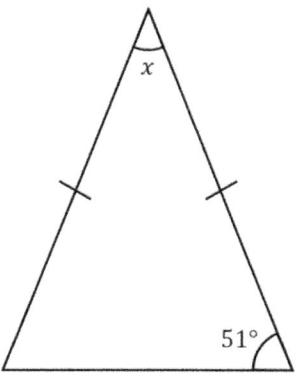

[2 marks]

31

Working space:

Test 10

Q1

What 3D shape can be constructed using the net shown below?

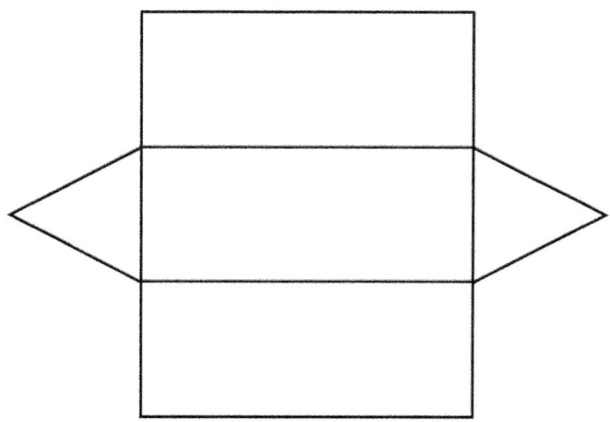

[1 mark]

Q2

Elise and Kyle both want to put some money in a savings account.

Elise is going to put £2500 into an account that offers her 3.6% compound interest paid annually.

Kyle is going to put £2600 into an account that offers him 2.4% simple interest paid annually.

Work out who has the most money in their respective savings account after 2 years.

[4 marks]

Q3

Rose has a dentist appointment at 10:15 am.

She sets off from her house at 9:15 am and walks to the bus stop, which is 1.6 km away, at an average speed of 5.5 km/h. The bus she wants to catch arrive at the bus stop every 15 minutes, with the first bus due at 8:00 am.

The bus then travels at an average speed of 24 km/h, for 8 km, at which point Rose gets off the bus.

She then walks for a further 0.9 km to the dentist, at an average speed of 4.5 km/h.

Does Rose get to her dentist appointment on time?

[3 marks]

Q4

On the axes below draw a straight line between the points $(-2, 3)$ and $(1, -5)$.

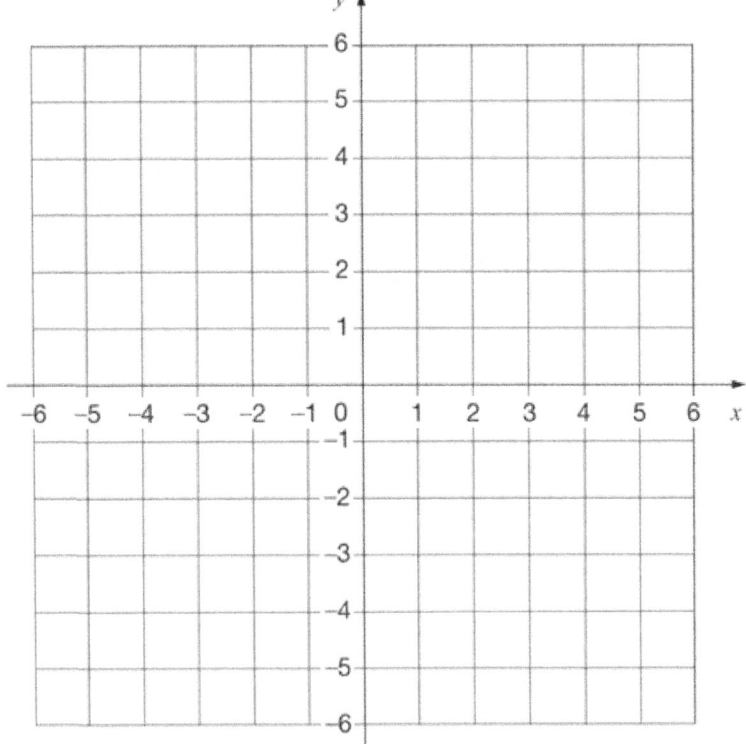

[2 marks]

Working space:

Test 11

Q1

Using the graph below, convert 15 lbs into kilograms

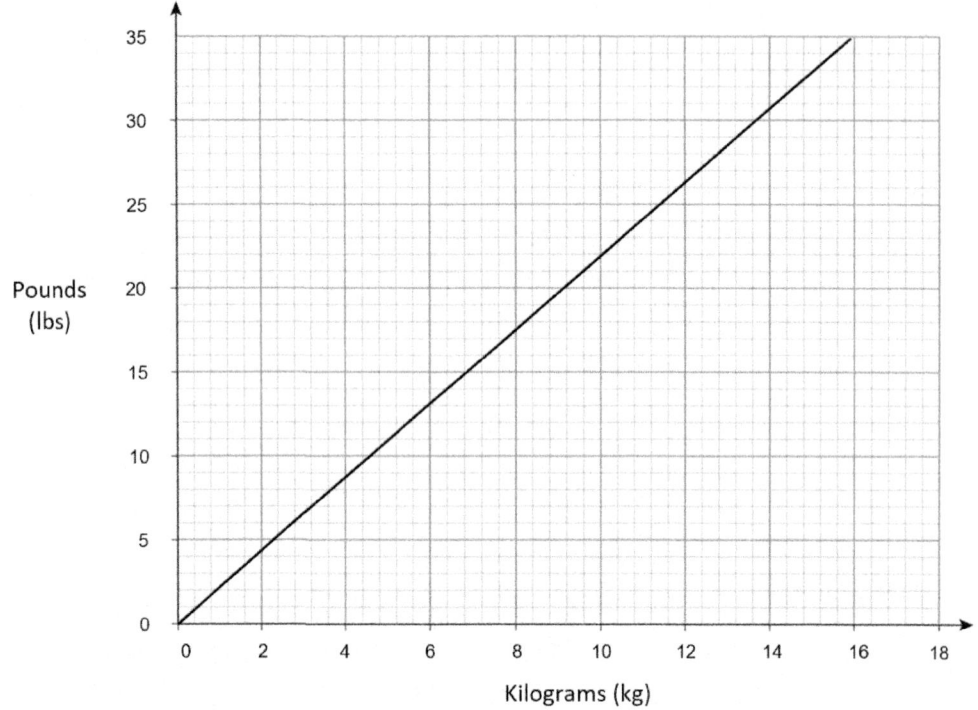

[1 mark]

Q2

The cylinder shown below has a diameter of 4.9 cm and a height of 6.2 cm.

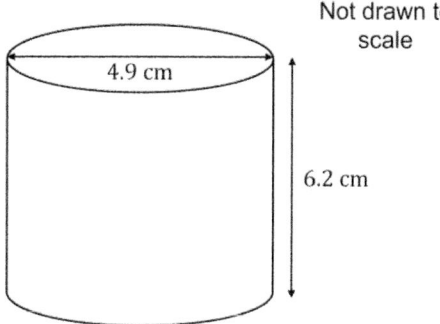

Calculate the volume of the cylinder, giving your answer to 2 decimal places.

Use $\pi = 3.14$

[2 marks]

Q3

The scale drawing below shows the plan view of a garden on centimetre square paper, containing a pond and a patio area. The remaining area of the garden will be turfed with grass.

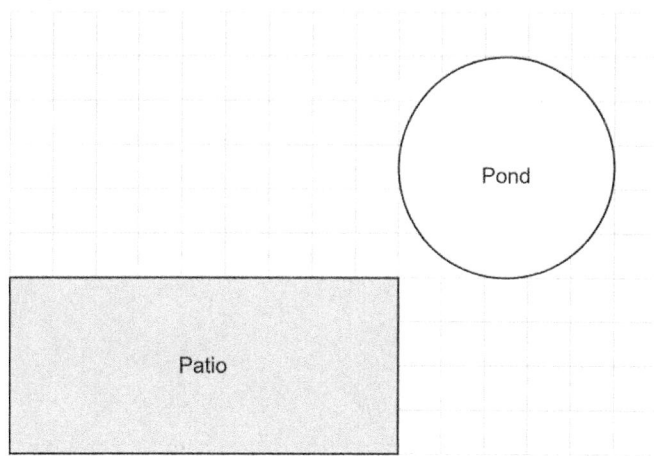

The grass turf is sold in rolls covering an area of 2 m², costing £7.35 per roll.

Given that the diagram uses a scale of 1 : 120, calculate the total cost of turfing the garden.

Use $\pi = 3.14$

[5 marks]

Q4

Draw the side elevation projection of the shape below.

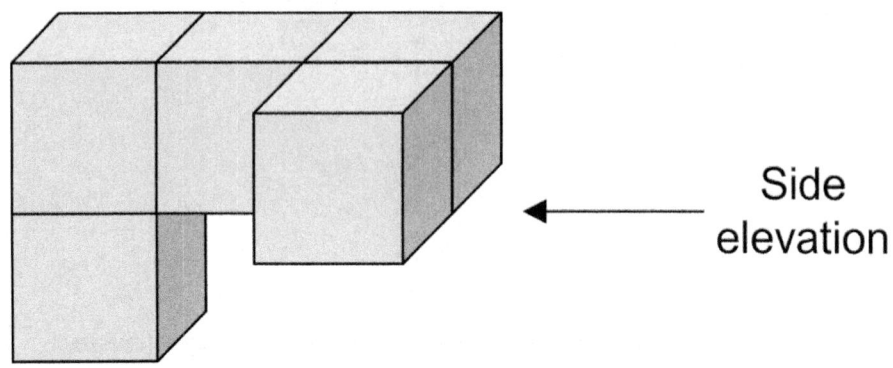

[1 mark]

Q5

The diagram below shows a quadrilateral.

Find angle x.

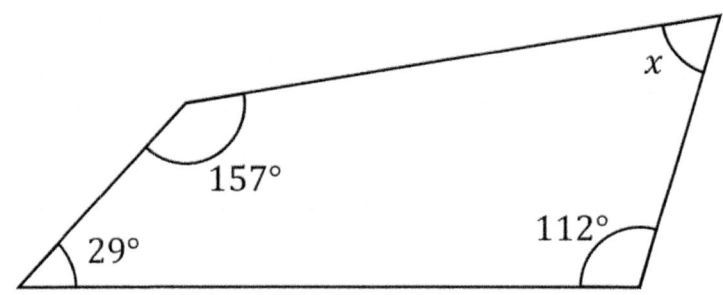

[1 mark]

Working space:

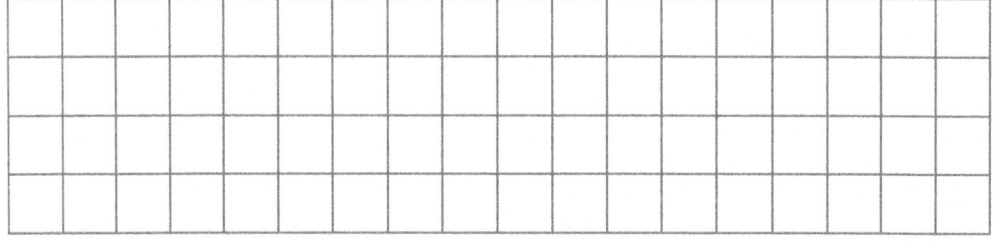

Test 12

Q1

Below is a circle with a radius of 5.3 cm.

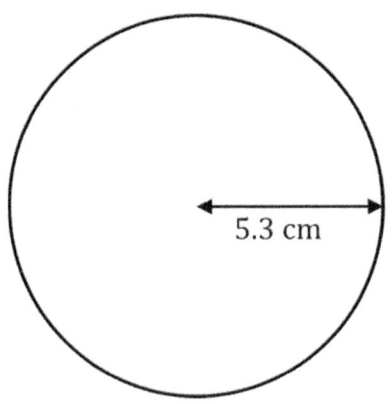

Calculate the circumference of the circle.

Use $\pi = 3.14$

[2 marks]

Q2

A school wants to buy a calculator for all 167 students in year 11.

They can choose from two suppliers shown below:

Maths Accessories	School Supplies
A box of 20 calculators for £90	£5.10 per calculator
Delivery cost: £3.50 per box	Free Delivery

Which supplier is better value for money for the school?

[4 marks]

Q3

Iron has a density of 7.87 g/cm^3.

Calculate the mass, in grams, of a 6 cm^3 lump of iron.

[2 marks]

Q4

Dorothy buys a house for 360000.

The house increases in value by 5.6% each year.

Calculate the value of the house after two years.

[2 marks]

Working space:

Test 13

Q1

Below is a diagram of a square-based pyramid.

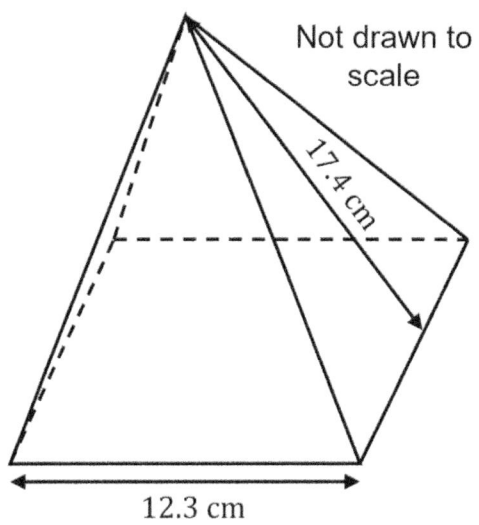

Not drawn to scale

17.4 cm

12.3 cm

Calculate the surface area of the pyramid.

[3 marks]

43

Q2

The diagram below shows the plan view of a floor, which is in the shape of a trapezium.

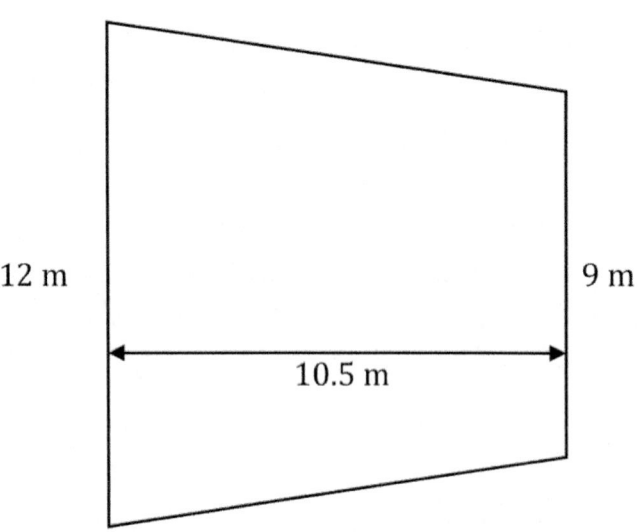

Sean is going to carpet the floor.

Each roll of carpet covers 4 m² and costs £18.50 per roll.

Sean has £500 to spend, does he have enough to buy all the carpet he needs for the floor?

Area of a trapezium = $\frac{a+b}{2} \times h$

where h = height and a and b are the widths of the trapezium at the top and bottom.

[4 marks]

Q3

Write down the coordinates of the point labelled A on the diagram below.

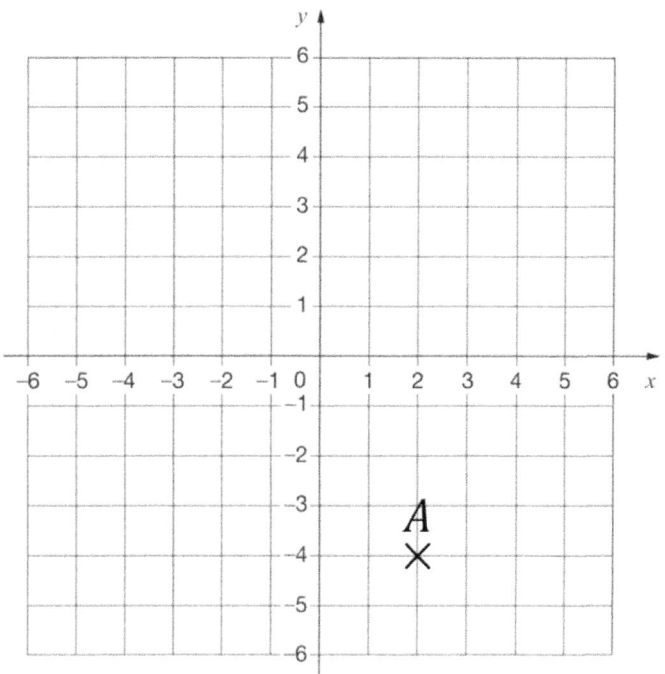

[1 mark]

Q4

Eve cycles 39 km in 1 hour and 45 minutes.

Calculate her average speed, giving your answer to 2 decimal places.

[2 marks]

Working space:

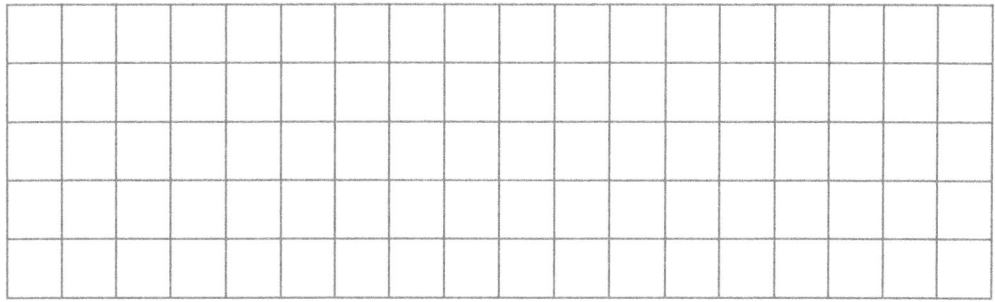

Test 14

Q1

Due to a constant increase in demand, the price of petrol increases by 5% every month.

If the price of petrol was £1.28 per litre in January, how much would it cost someone to buy 30 litres of petrol in April?

[3 marks]

Q2

Daniel buys 6 packets of collectable cards, which cost £1.95 each.

He keeps them in pristine condition for 15 years and then sells the whole collection for £142.

Calculate the percentage profit in selling the cards, giving your answer to 1 decimal place.

[3 marks]

Q3

What is the name of this 3D shape?

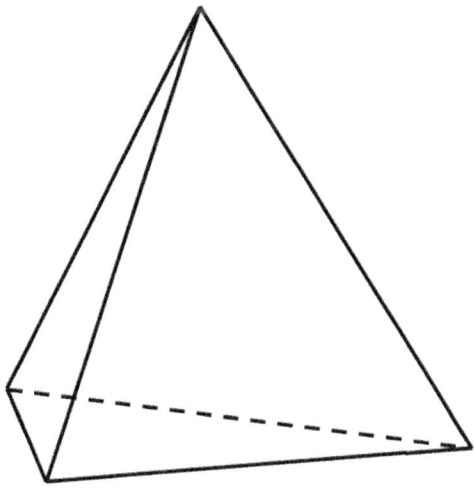

[1 mark]

Q4

A pizza in the shape of a circle that has a diameter of 16 inches, is cut into 8 equal slices. Calculate the perimeter of one slice of pizza.

Use π = 3.14

[3 marks]

Working space:

Test 15

Q1

Draw a front elevation and side elevation of the shape below.

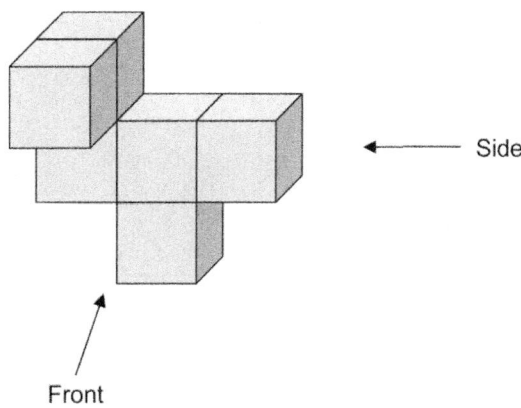

[2 marks]

Q2

On the grid below, plot the points $(-5, 4)$, $(1, 4)$ and $(1, -1)$.

Connect the points and find the area of the shape that is formed.

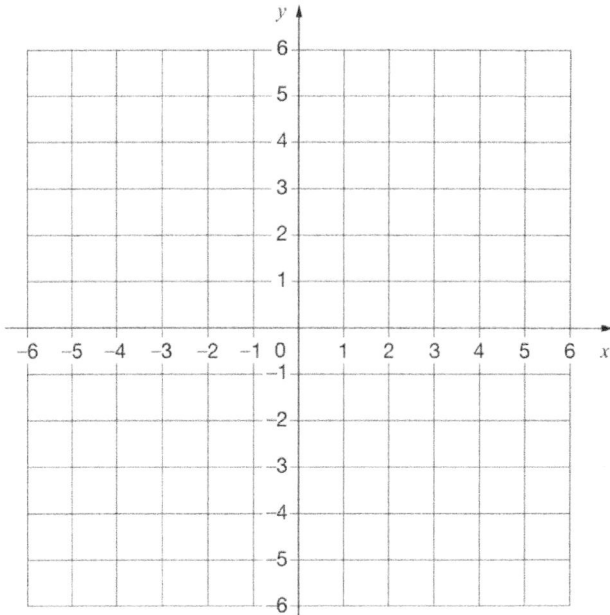

[3 marks]

Q3

Calculate the surface area of the cuboid shown below.

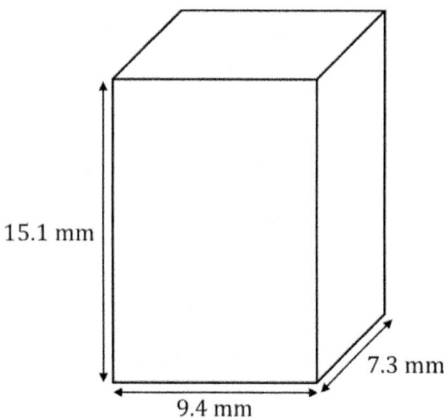

[3 marks]

Q4

Calculate the perimeter of the shape below.

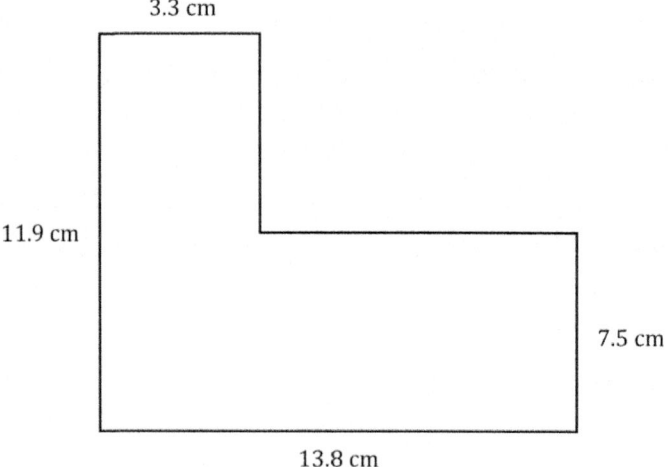

[2 marks]

Working space:

Test 16

Q1

The diagram below shows 4 equally sized circles inside a square.

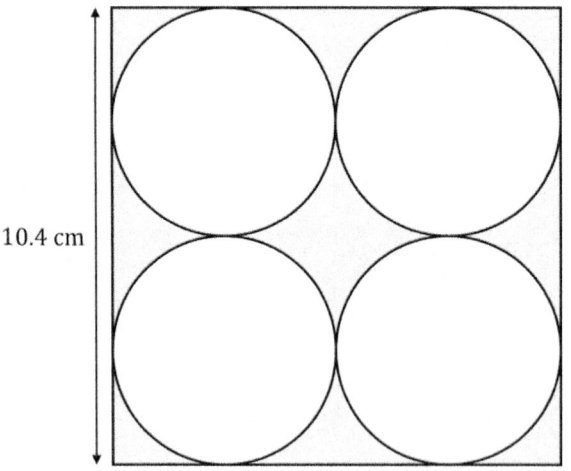

10.4 cm

Calculate the area of the shaded region.

Use $\pi = 3.14$

[4 marks]

Q2

Calculate the distance between Belfast and Newcastle using the scale map below.

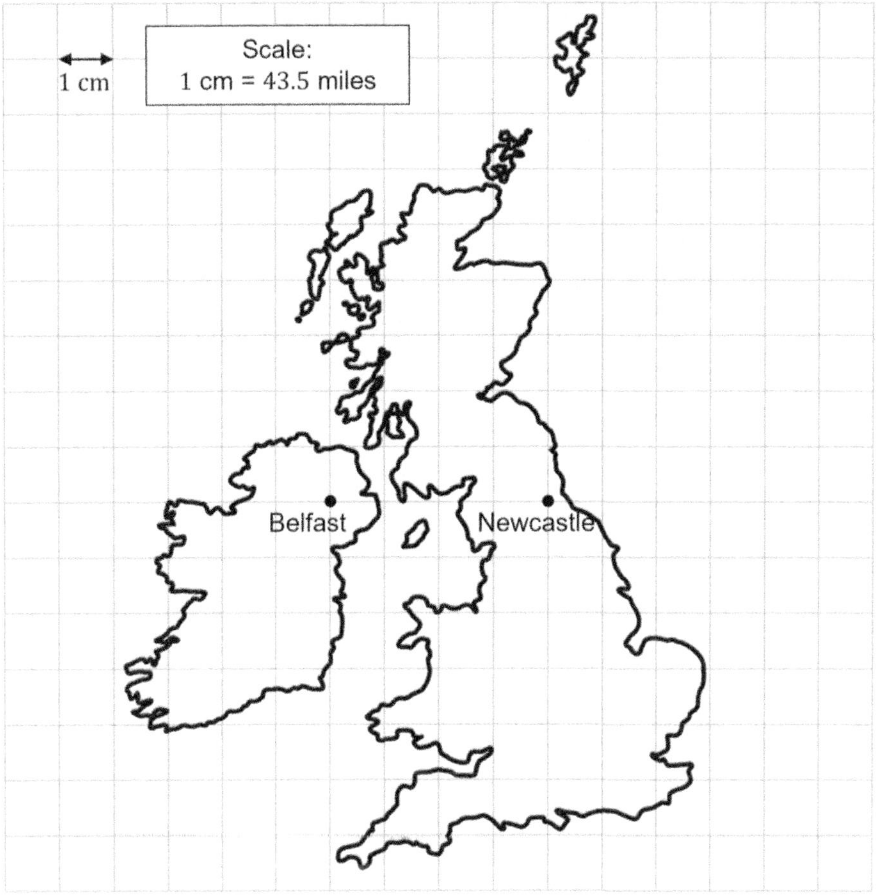

Scale: 1 cm = 43.5 miles

[2 marks]

Q3

Calculate the angle x.

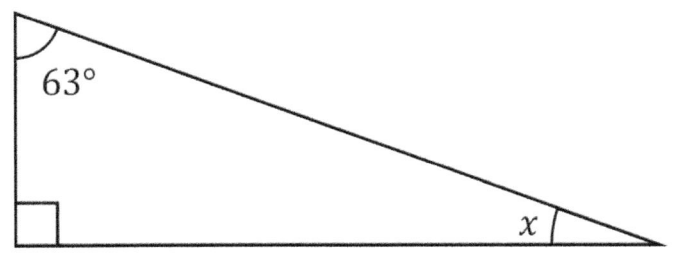

[2 marks]

Q4

Using the conversion graph below, convert 27 metres into feet.

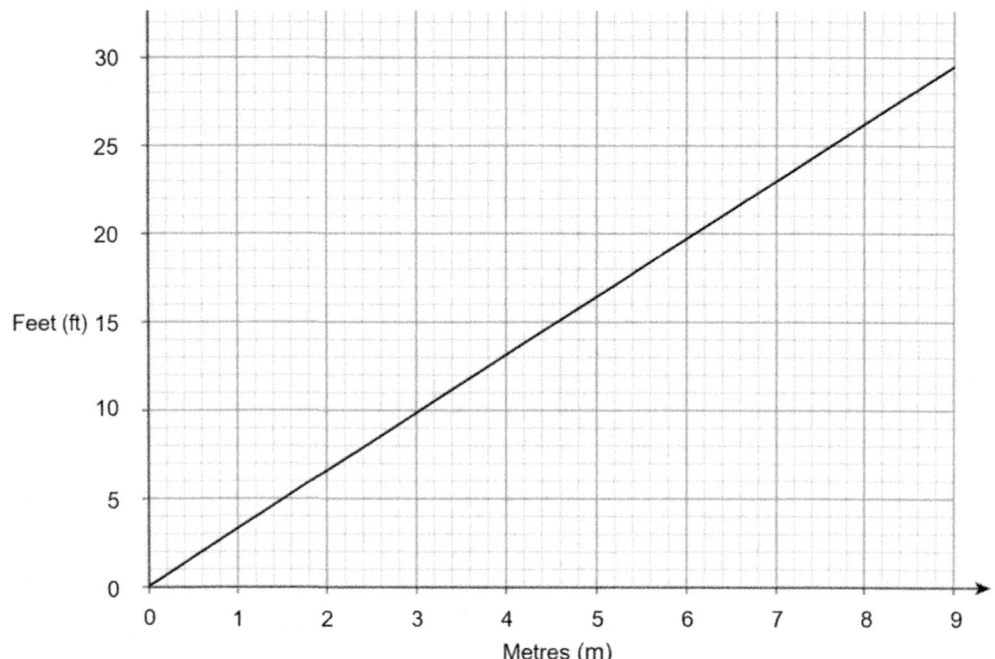

[2 marks]

Working space:

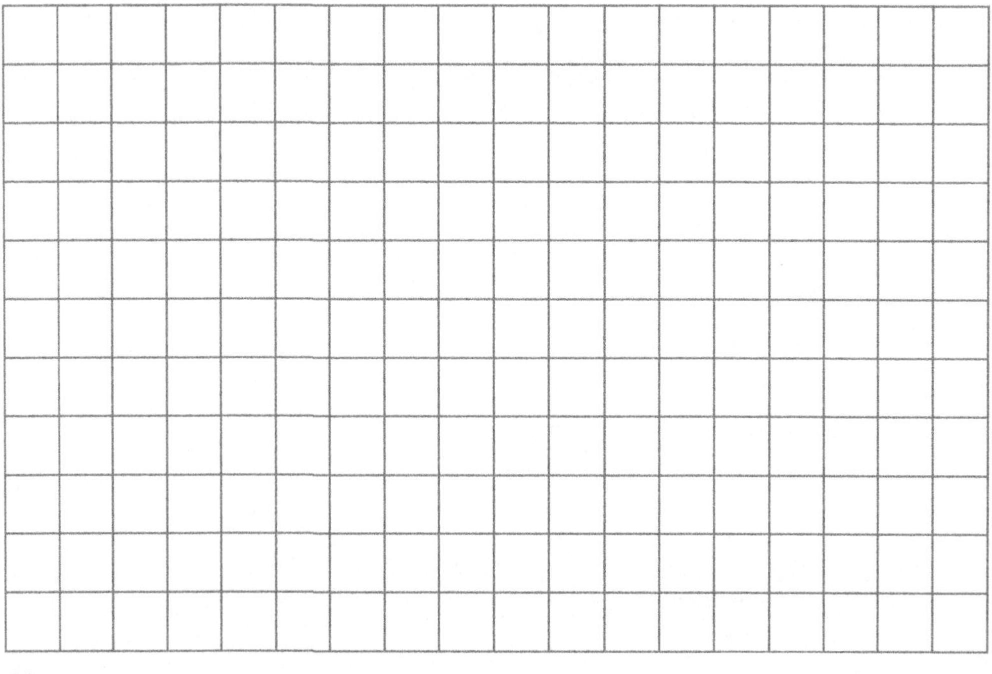

Functional Skills Maths Level 2
Revision Fundamentals

Practice Paper Bundle

- ✓ **20** unique functional skills maths level 2 **practice papers** & **mark schemes**
- ✓ **Recommended** by **tutors** and **colleges**
- ✓ **Designed** by **experts**

Revision Cards

- ✓ **Recommended** by **students** and **tutors**
- ✓ Relevant to **all exam boards**
- ✓ Covers **all topics** in your exam

Revision Card and Practice Paper Bundle

- ✓ Papers from the **exam board** of your choice
- ✓ **Explanations, practice questions** and **exam questions** on every topic
- ✓ **Save** with the bundle **discount**

Fill your boots...
...with essential **revision supplies**!

Get prepared at pfs.la/shop

Handling Information and Data

 Test 17

Q1

Calculate the mean of the following numbers:

0.8,　1.6,　2.3,　1.5,　1.2,　1.4,　1.9,　1.7

[2 marks]

Q2

Rick rolls a fair six-sided die, numbered 1, 2, 3, 4, 5 and 6.

What is the probability that he rolls an even number?

[1 mark]

Q3

The incomplete table below shows information about the favourite subject of students in year 7, 8 and 9 out of maths, English, and science.

Year	Subject			Total
	Maths	English	Science	
7	24		35	136
8		52		142
9			61	
Total	99	189		420

Complete the table.

[3 marks]

Q4

The table below shows information on the average daily temperature and the number of bottles of sun cream sold at a shop over 10 days.

Average temperature (°C)	Sun cream bottles sold
22	5
18	2
24	6
17	1
21	4
25	9
20	7
19	2
23	5

Plot this information on a scatter graph on the set of axes below.

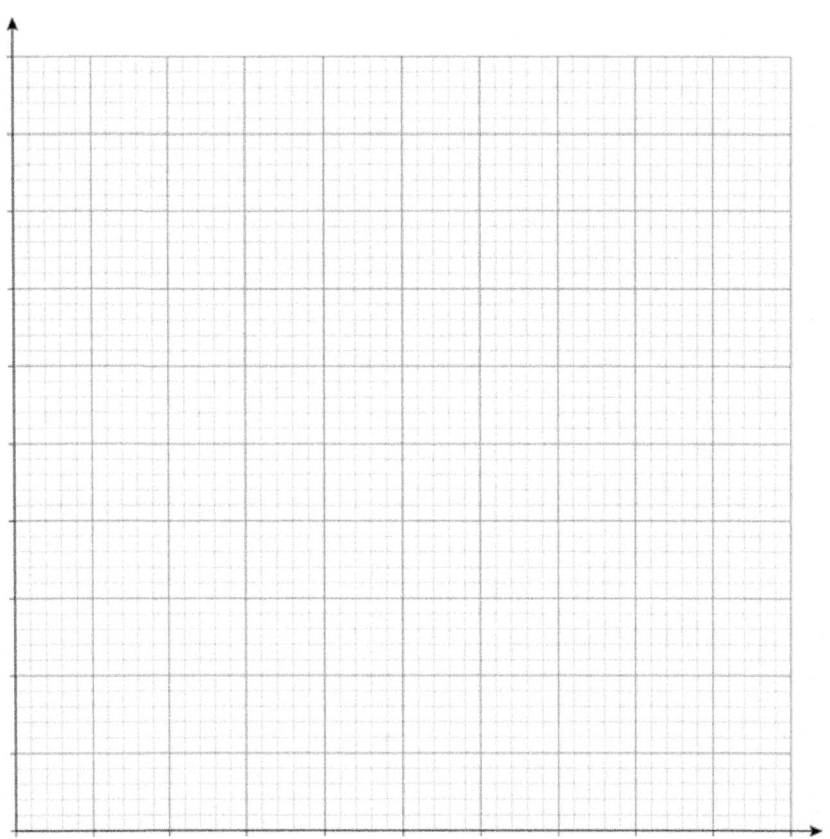

[4 marks]

Working space:

Test 18

Q1

Florence works at a cinema and records the ages of people going to see a new superhero film.

She records this information in the table below.

Age (years)	Frequency
0 – 10	9
11 – 17	22
18 – 30	26
31 – 55	11
56 – 75	6
76 – 100	2

Estimate the mean age of the people who watched the film, giving your answer to the nearest year.

[4 marks]

Q2

Calculate the median and mode of the following numbers:

$$7, 4, 6, 9, 11, 8, 3, 4, 5, 10, 6, 8, 4, 2$$

[2 marks]

Q3

Chris has a bag with 20 counters in it.

There are 7 blue counters, 8 red counters and 5 yellow counters in the bag.

Chris randomly selects a counter from the bag, notes down the colour and then replaces it. He then randomly selects another counter and notes down the colour.

Calculate the probability that the counters that he selected from the bag were both yellow.

[2 marks]

Q4

A teacher records the scores that students got in an English exam and wants to compare the boys' scores against the girls' scores.

Using the information in the table below, who had the more consistent scores, the boys, or the girls?

	Exam Score									
Boys	74	68	87	83	71	56	64	79	58	78
Girls	91	78	61	55	72	83	68	85	74	51

[2 marks]

Working space:

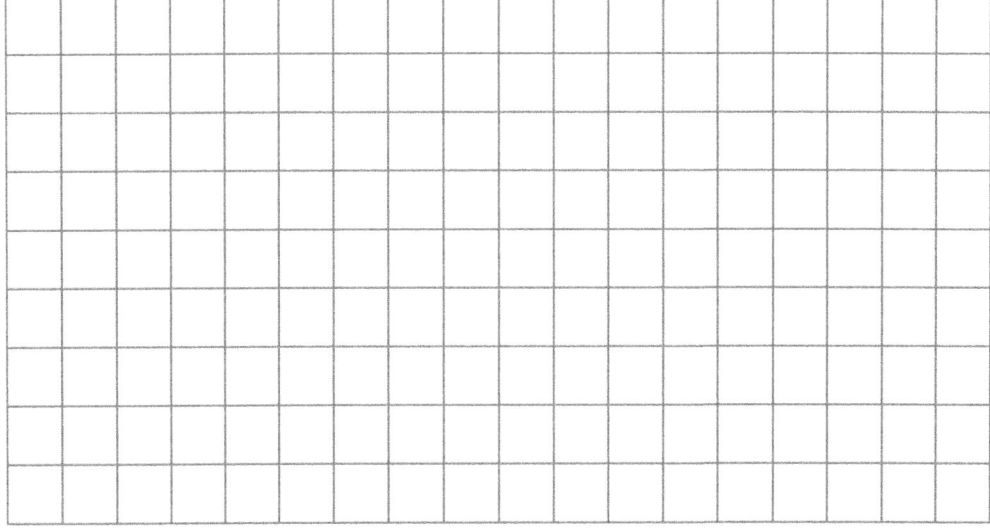

Test 19

Q1

Describe the correlation in the scatter graph below.

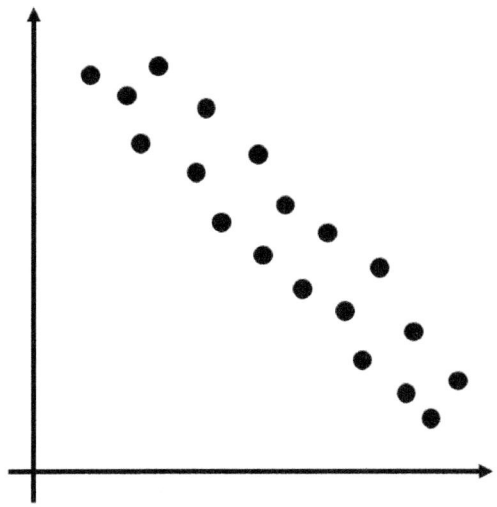

[1 mark]

Q2

The table below shows information about the number of customers a burger van had between 12:00 pm and 2:00 pm every day for a two-week period.

	Number of customers						
	Monday	Tuesday	Wednesday	Thursday	Friday	Saturday	Sunday
Week 1	8	11	7	6	10	9	12
Week 2	10	12	5	11	7	13	6

Which week had a higher average number of customers?

[3 marks]

Q3

A class sat a history test and a geography test.

Their scores are represented on the scatter graph below.

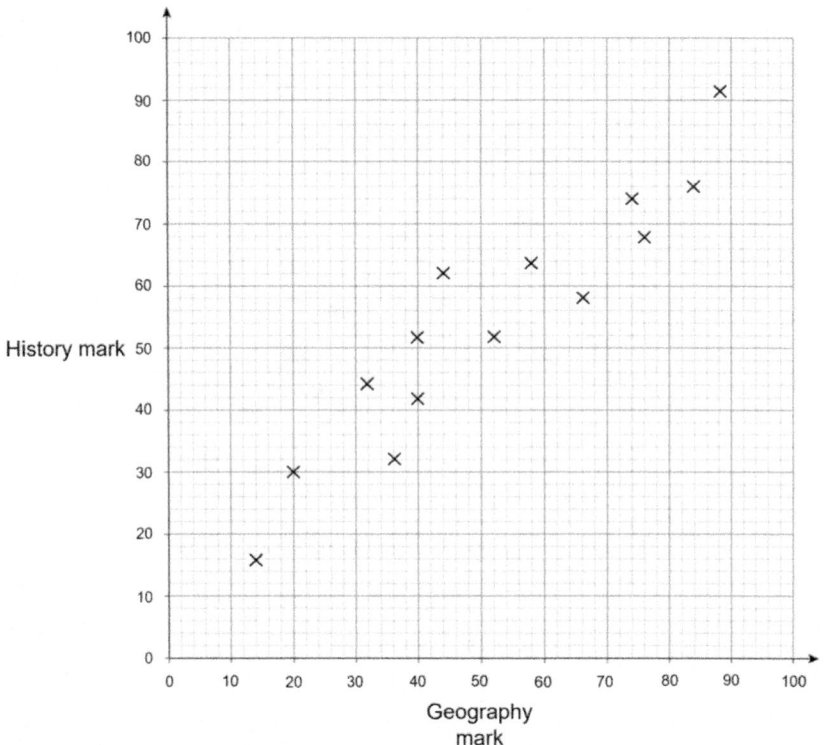

Draw a line of best fit on the scatter graph.

[1 mark]

Q4

The table below shows the average time five friends spent on their mobile phones on two different weeks.

Name	Screen time (minutes)	
	Week 1	Week 2
Peter	258	312
Rosie	315	299
Aaron	185	181
Brooke	171	203
Phoebe	199	212

Calculate the difference in the mean screen time between week 1 and week 2.

[3 marks]

Q5

The probabilities of a spinner landing on each of its three different colours are shown in the incomplete table below.

Colour	Blue	Green	Red
Probability	0.25	0.3	

The spinner is spun twice, by completing the table calculate the probability that the spinner lands on red both times.

[2 marks]

Working space:

Test 20

Q1

The table below shows the commute time for employees of a company.

Commute time (minutes)	Frequency
1 – 10	6
11 – 20	16
21 – 30	21
31 – 40	11
41 – 50	4
51 – 60	2

Estimate the mean commute time for employees of this company.

[4 marks]

Q2

Tristan flips an unbiased coin three times, calculate the probability that it lands on heads all three times.

[1 mark]

Q3

The table below shows information about the average possession and goals scored of some football teams.

Average Possession (%)	Goals Scored
54	55
51	40
42	33
40	41
50	27
58	62
62	68
64	76
52	68
38	35

Represent this data on a scatter graph using the set of axes below.

Draw a line of best fit and describe the correlation.

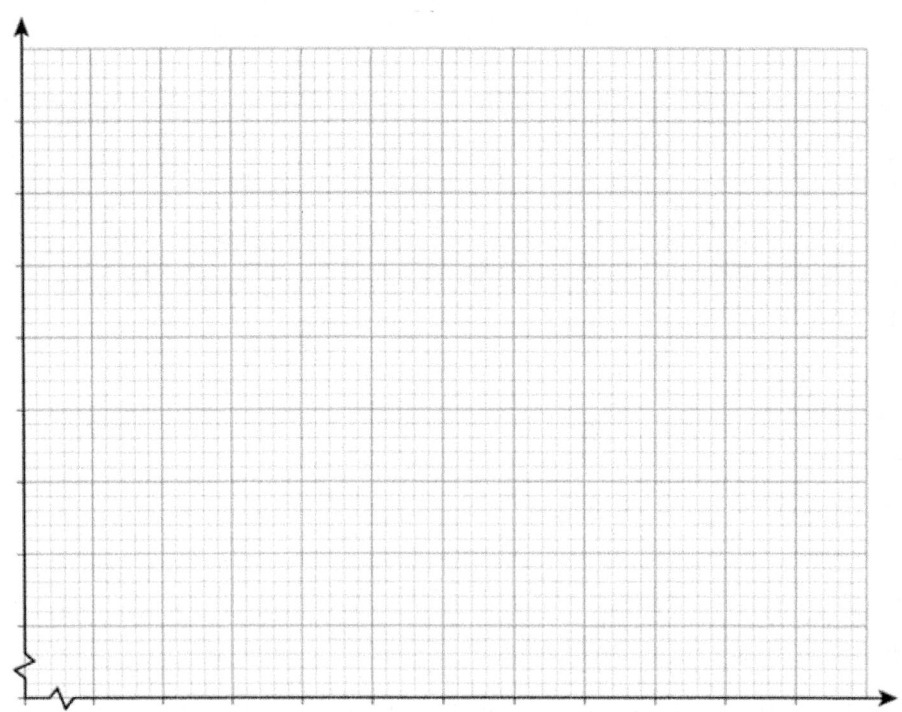

[5 marks]

Working space:

Functional Skills Maths Level 2 Course

You are unique...

 Virtual **exam mocks**

 **Personalised** topic recommendations

 Detailed **video explanations**

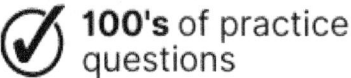 **100's** of practice questions

 Learn on **your own** schedule

 **Expertly designed** course

Shouldn't your learning be too?

Get learning at pfs.la/courses

Answers

	Using Numbers	
	Test 1	
Q1	$-2.710, -2.701, -2.071, 0.207, 2.017$	[1]
Q2	56.847	[1]
Q3	$\dfrac{13}{6} - \dfrac{7}{4} = \dfrac{26}{12} - \dfrac{21}{12}$	[1]
	$\dfrac{5}{12}$	[1]
Q4	For rounding all the numbers e.g. $\dfrac{12 \times 2}{5+3}$	[1]
	3 (Allow alternative answers from correct first step)	[1]
Q5	Attempt to use the column or grid method	[1]
	8862	[1]
Q6	$40 \text{ g} \div 2 = 20 \text{ g}$ (One part)	[1]
	$20 \text{ g} \times 6 = 120 \text{ g}$ (Amount of flour for 12 cupcakes)	[1]
	$120 \text{ g} \times 2 = 240 \text{ g}$	[1]
	Test 2	
Q1	Writing all fractions with a common denominator e.g. $\dfrac{16}{36}, \dfrac{15}{36}, \dfrac{12}{36}, \dfrac{27}{36}$	[1]
	$\dfrac{1}{3}, \dfrac{5}{12}, \dfrac{4}{9}, \dfrac{3}{4}$	[1]
Q2	17	[1]
Q3	35%	[1]
Q4	68	[1]

Q5	$10 \times 12 - 10 \times 4 = 80$	[1]
	$80 \div 8 = 10$	[1]
	10	[1]
Q6	$\frac{7}{10} \times £50 = £35$ **or** $1 - \frac{7}{10} = \frac{3}{10}$	[1]
	£15	[1]
Test 3		
Q1	10% of £84 = £8.40 or 84 × 0.3	[1]
	£25.20	[1]
Q2	0.03 or 3 hundredths	[1]
Q3	Process to find 15% of £420 e.g. $42 + 21 = 63$ **or** 0.15×420 **Or** process to find 85% of £420 e.g. $8 \times 42 + 21$ or 0.85×420	[1]
	£357	[1]
Q4	$70 \div (9 + 5) = 5$	[1]
	Alice: $9 \times 5 = £45$ Brandon: $5 \times 5 = £25$	[1]
	40% of £45 = £18 60% of £25 = £15	[1]
	6 : 5	[1]
Q5	120.75	[1]

	Test 4	
Q1	$\dfrac{240-150}{150}$	[1]
	60%	[1]
Q2	$\dfrac{3}{20}$	[1]
Q3	£9.87 and £12.34 correctly rounded to £10 and £12 respectively	[1]
	£10 × 28 + £12 × 6 (Allow rounded values for 28 and 6)	[1]
	£352 (Allow correct answer from different correct estimates)	[1]
Q4	23.5	[1]
Q5	3 × 10 = 30 (One person)	[1]
	30 ÷ 5	[1]
	6 days	[1]
	Test 5	
Q1	−4	[1]
Q2	60	[1]
Q3	£1890 ÷ 3 = £630 £1650 ÷ 3 = £550	[1]
	£630 ÷ 3 × 10 = £2100 £550 × 4 = £2200	[1]
	Carrie (with correct supported figures)	[1]
Q4	$\dfrac{2}{9}+\dfrac{3}{5}=\dfrac{10}{45}+\dfrac{27}{45}$	[1]
	$\dfrac{37}{45}$	[1]
Q5	1430208	[1]

Q6	$\frac{3}{8}$ of £60 = £22.50 or $\frac{4}{7}$ of £42 = £24	[1]
	Gwen (with correct supporting figures)	[1]
Test 6		
Q1	£4760 ÷ 0.85 or £4670 × 100 ÷ 85	[1]
	£5600	[1]
Q2	20 or twenty or 2 tens	[1]
Q3	Scale factor $\frac{20}{8}$ = 2.5 or method to work out ingredients needed for 1 pancake e.g., 100 ÷ 8 (= 12.5)	[1]
	Method to work out amount needed for one of the ingredients to make 20 pancakes e.g., 100 × 2.5 (= 250) or 12.5 × 20 (= 250)	[1]
	250 g of flour 5 large eggs 750 ml of milk	[1]
Q4	17.5%	[1]
Q5	No. of bars in one box = 25 × 12 = 300	[1]
	No. of boxes needed = 1600 ÷ 300 = 5.33 ...	[1]
	6 boxes	[1]
Test 7		
Q1	$\frac{6}{13} + \frac{7}{8} = \frac{48}{104} + \frac{91}{104}$	[1]
	$\frac{139}{104}$ or $1\frac{35}{104}$	[1]
Q2	$\frac{449-499}{499}$ or $\frac{499-449}{499}$	[1]
	10.02%	[1]

Q3	$V = \frac{4}{3} \times 3.14 \times 3.8^3$ or $V = \frac{4}{3} \times 3.14 \times 3.8 \times 3.8 \times 3.8$	[1]
	229.73	[1]
	cm³	[1]
Q4	0.10031, 0.01313, 0.01303, 0.01033, 0.00301	[1]
Q5	$4 + 5 + 8 = 17$ **and** $51 \div 17 = 3$	[1]
	Nathan: $4 \times 3 = 12$ years old Isabella: $5 \times 3 = 15$ years old Tanya: $8 \times 3 = 24$ years old	[1]
Test 8		
Q1	Cost of one bike: £5 + 6 × £3.50 + £2.50 = £28.50	[1]
	£57	[1]
Q2	$2\frac{2}{7} - 1\frac{3}{4} = 2\frac{8}{28} - 1\frac{21}{28}$	[1]
	$\frac{15}{28}$	[1]
Q3	$\frac{1}{8} = 12.5\%$	[1]
	Digital Age - £211.65	[1]
Q4	12000 m² ÷ (8 × 6) = 250 m² (Turf laid in one day by one worker)	[1]
	30000 m² − 12000 m² = 18000 m²	[1]
	18000 m² ÷ 2 = 9000 m² **and** 9000 ÷ 250 = 36 workers needed for the remaining 2 days	[1]
	36 − 6 = 30 additional workers	[1]

Common Measures, Shape and Space

Test 9

Q1	$134 \div 1.30$	[1]
	£103.08	[1]
Q2	$11.2 + 11.2 + 7.45 + 7.45$	[1]
	37.3	[1]
Q3	Area of triangle = $4.25 \times 4.25 \times 0.5 (= 9.03125)$	[1]
	Area of circle = $3.14 \times 4.25 \times 4.25 (= 56.71625)$	[1]
	"56.71625" − "9.03125"	[1]
	47.685 cm²	[1]
Q4	$180 - (2 \times 51)$	[1]
	78°	[1]

Test 10

Q1	Triangular Prism	[1]
Q2	Elise after 1 year = £2500 × 1.036 = £2590	[1]
	Elise after 2 years = £2590 × 1.036 = £2683.24	[1]
	Kyle after 2 years = £2600 × 1.048 = £2724.80	[1]
	Kyle (with correct supporting figures)	[1]
Q3	Time taken to get to the bus stop $= \frac{1.6}{5.5} \times 60 = 17.45$ minutes So, she catches the 9:45 am bus.	[1]
	Time spent on the bus $= \frac{8}{24} \times 60 = 20$ minutes So, she gets off the bus at 10:05 am. and Time spent walking $= \frac{0.9}{4.5} \times 60 = 12$ minutes	[1]
	No (with supported figures e.g., arrive at 10:17 am)	[1]

Q4	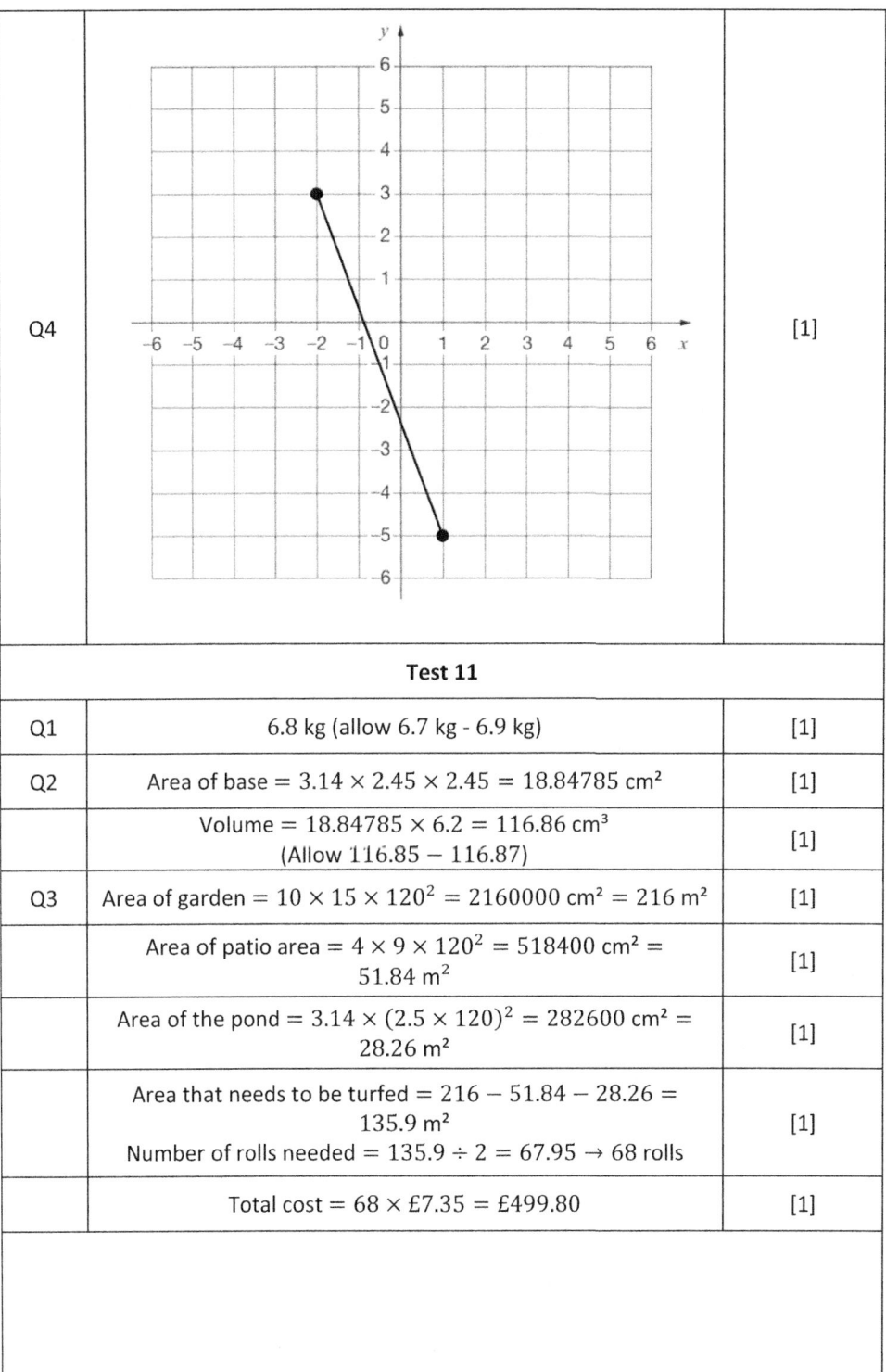		[1]

	Test 11		
Q1	6.8 kg (allow 6.7 kg - 6.9 kg)		[1]
Q2	Area of base = $3.14 \times 2.45 \times 2.45 = 18.84785$ cm²		[1]
	Volume = $18.84785 \times 6.2 = 116.86$ cm³ (Allow $116.85 - 116.87$)		[1]
Q3	Area of garden = $10 \times 15 \times 120^2 = 2160000$ cm² = 216 m²		[1]
	Area of patio area = $4 \times 9 \times 120^2 = 518400$ cm² = 51.84 m²		[1]
	Area of the pond = $3.14 \times (2.5 \times 120)^2 = 282600$ cm² = 28.26 m²		[1]
	Area that needs to be turfed = $216 - 51.84 - 28.26 = 135.9$ m² Number of rolls needed = $135.9 \div 2 = 67.95 \rightarrow 68$ rolls		[1]
	Total cost = $68 \times £7.35 = £499.80$		[1]

Q4		[1]
Q5	$360° - 112° - 157° - 29° = 62°$	[1]
Test 12		
Q1	$3.14 \times (5.3 \times 2)$	[1]
	33.284	[1]
Q2	Maths Accessories: $167 \div 20 = 8.35 \rightarrow 9$ boxes needed	[1]
	Total cost for Maths Accessories $= 9 \times (£90 + £3.50) = £841.50$	[1]
	School Supplies total cost $= 167 \times £5.10 = £851.70$	[1]
	Maths Accessories (with supported figures)	[1]
Q3	7.87×6 **or** mass = density × volume	[1]
	47.22 g	[1]
Q4	After 1 year: $\$360000 \times 1.056 = \$380160$	[1]
	After 2 years: $\$380160 \times 1.056 = \$401448.96$	[1]
Test 13		
Q1	Area of square base $= 12.3 \times 12.3 = 151.29$ cm²	[1]
	Area of one triangular side $= \frac{1}{2} \times 17.4 \times 12.3 = 107.01$ cm²	[1]
	Surface area $= 4 \times 107.01 + 151.29 = 579.33$ cm²	[1]
Q2	Area of the floor $= \frac{12+9}{2} \times 10.5 = 110.25$ m²	[1]
	$110.25 \div 4 = 27.5625 \rightarrow 28$ rolls	[1]
	Total cost: $28 \times £18.50 = £518$	[1]
	Sean doesn't have enough (with supported figures)	[1]

Q3	$(2, -4)$		[1]
Q4	1 hour 45 mins = 1.75 hours or speed = $\frac{\text{distance}}{\text{time}}$		[1]
	$\frac{39}{1.75} = 22.29$ km/h		[1]

Test 14

Q1	£1.28 × 1.05 = £1.34(4) – after one month	[1]
	£1.28 × 1.05 × 1.05 × 1.05 = £1.48 – price in April	[1]
	£1.48 × 30 = £44.40 (Allow £1.48176 × 30 = £44.45)	[1]
Q2	6 × £1.95 = £11.70	[1]
	$\frac{142 - 11.70}{11.70} \times 100$	[1]
	1113.7%	[1]
Q3	Triangle-based pyramid or tetrahedron	[1]
Q4	Circumference of whole pizza = 3.14 × 16 = 50.24 inches	[1]
	$\frac{50.24}{8} + 8 + 8$	[1]
	22.28 inches	[1]

Test 15

Q1	Front:	[1]
	Side:	[1]

Q2	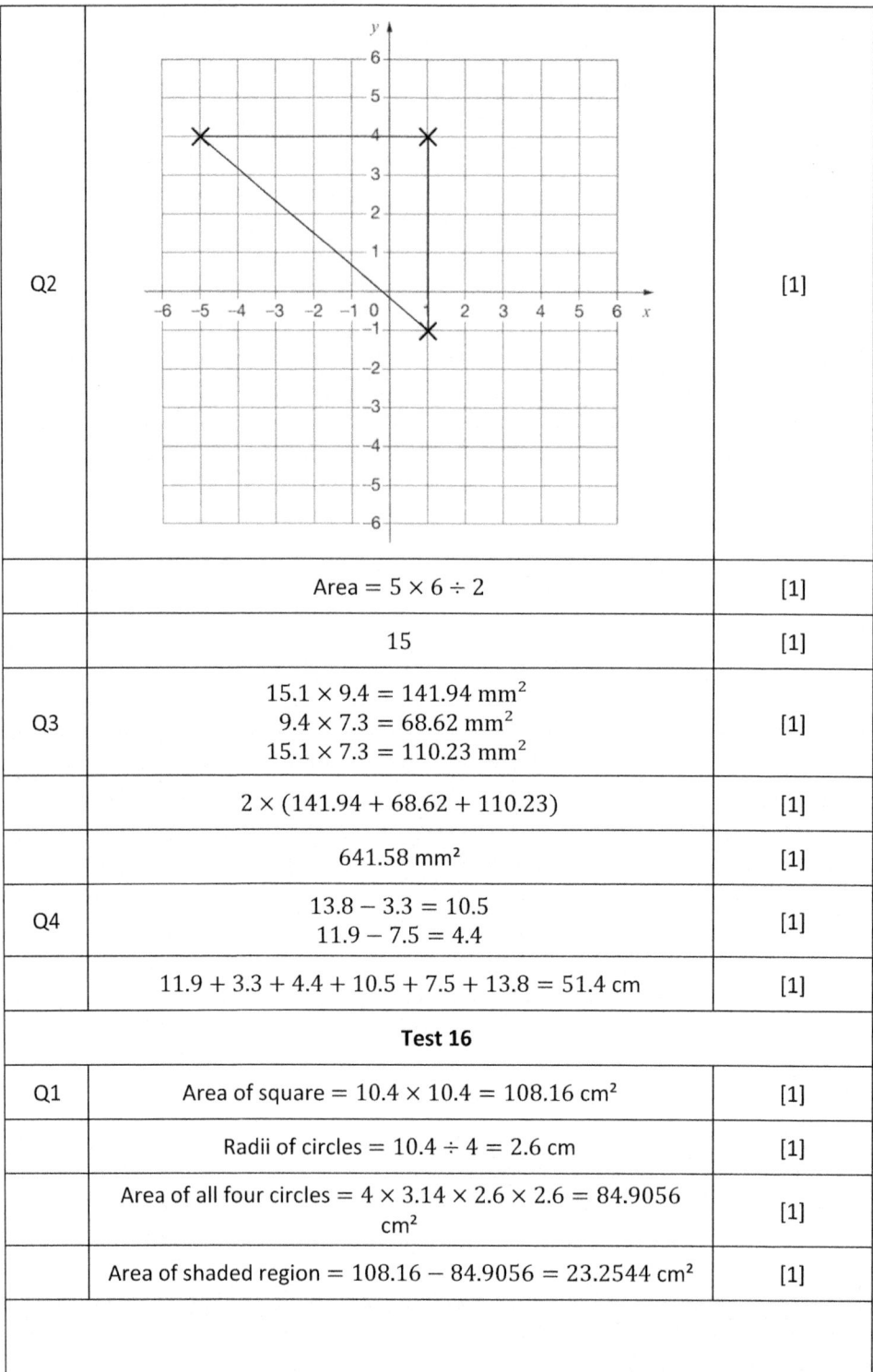	[1]
	Area = $5 \times 6 \div 2$	[1]
	15	[1]
Q3	$15.1 \times 9.4 = 141.94$ mm² $9.4 \times 7.3 = 68.62$ mm² $15.1 \times 7.3 = 110.23$ mm²	[1]
	$2 \times (141.94 + 68.62 + 110.23)$	[1]
	641.58 mm²	[1]
Q4	$13.8 - 3.3 = 10.5$ $11.9 - 7.5 = 4.4$	[1]
	$11.9 + 3.3 + 4.4 + 10.5 + 7.5 + 13.8 = 51.4$ cm	[1]

Test 16

Q1	Area of square = $10.4 \times 10.4 = 108.16$ cm²	[1]
	Radii of circles = $10.4 \div 4 = 2.6$ cm	[1]
	Area of all four circles = $4 \times 3.14 \times 2.6 \times 2.6 = 84.9056$ cm²	[1]
	Area of shaded region = $108.16 - 84.9056 = 23.2544$ cm²	[1]

Q2	43.5×4	[1]
	174 miles	[1]
Q3	$180 - 90 - 63$	[1]
	$27°$	[1]
Q4	$3\text{ m} = 10\text{ ft}$	[1]
	90 feet (Allow 88 – 92)	[1]

Handling Information and Data

Test 17

Q1	$\dfrac{0.8 + 1.6 + 2.3 + 1.5 + 1.2 + 1.4 + 1.9 + 1.7}{8}$	[1]
	1.55	[1]
Q2	0.5 or $\dfrac{1}{2}$ or 50%	[1]
Q3	<table><tr><th rowspan="2">Year</th><th colspan="4">Subject</th></tr><tr><th>Maths</th><th>English</th><th>Science</th><th>Total</th></tr><tr><td>7</td><td>24</td><td>77</td><td>35</td><td>136</td></tr><tr><td>8</td><td>54</td><td>52</td><td>36</td><td>142</td></tr><tr><td>9</td><td>21</td><td>60</td><td>61</td><td>142</td></tr><tr><td>Total</td><td>99</td><td>189</td><td>132</td><td>420</td></tr></table>	[3] (2 correct figures – 1 mark) (4 correct figures – 2 marks) (All figures needed for 3 marks)

Q4	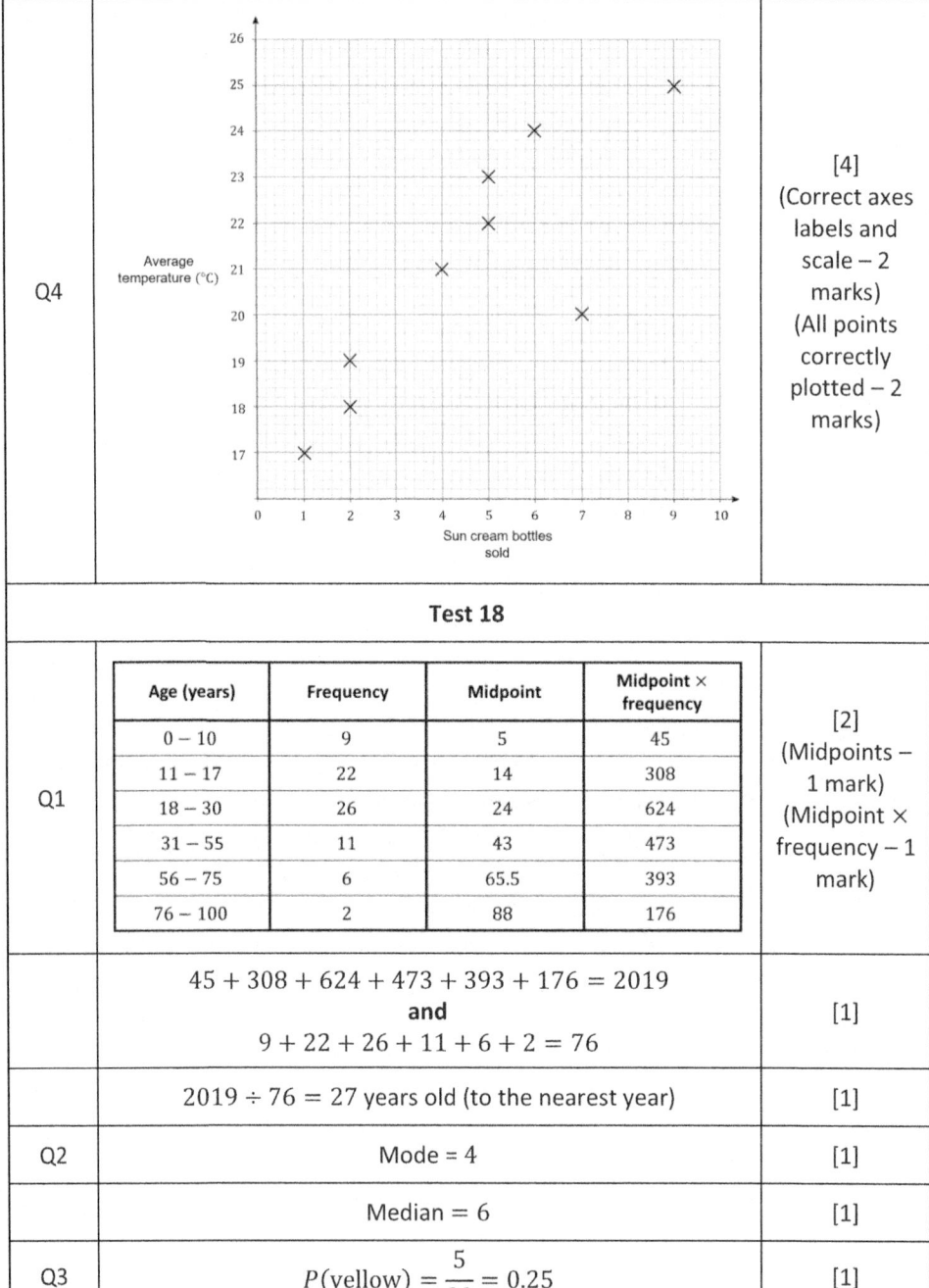	[4] (Correct axes labels and scale – 2 marks) (All points correctly plotted – 2 marks)

Test 18

Q1	Age (years)	Frequency	Midpoint	Midpoint × frequency	[2] (Midpoints – 1 mark) (Midpoint × frequency – 1 mark)
	0 – 10	9	5	45	
	11 – 17	22	14	308	
	18 – 30	26	24	624	
	31 – 55	11	43	473	
	56 – 75	6	65.5	393	
	76 – 100	2	88	176	

	$45 + 308 + 624 + 473 + 393 + 176 = 2019$ **and** $9 + 22 + 26 + 11 + 6 + 2 = 76$	[1]
	$2019 \div 76 = 27$ years old (to the nearest year)	[1]
Q2	Mode = 4	[1]
	Median = 6	[1]
Q3	$P(\text{yellow}) = \dfrac{5}{20} = 0.25$	[1]
	$0.25 \times 0.25 = 0.0625$ or $\dfrac{1}{16}$ or 6.25%	[1]

Q4	Range for boys = 87 − 56 = 31 **or** Range for girls = 91 − 51 = 40	[1]
	Boys (with ranges for boys and girls found)	[1]
Test 19			
Q1	Negative	[1]
Q2	Week 1: $\frac{8+11+7+6+10+9+12}{7} = 9$	[1]
	Week 2: $\frac{10+12+5+11+7+13+6}{7} = 9.142\ldots$	[1]
	Week 2 (with supported figures)	[1]
Q3	 (scatter graph of History mark vs Geography mark with line of best fit)	[1] (Roughly equal number of points either side of the line, going through as many as possible)
Q4	Week 1: $\frac{258+315+185+171+199}{5} = 225.6$ minutes	[1]
	Week 2: $\frac{312+299+181+203+212}{5} = 241.4$ minutes	[1]
	$241.4 - 225.6 = 15.8$ minutes	[1]
Q5	P(Red) = 0.45	[1]
	$0.45 \times 0.45 = 0.2025$	[1]

Test 20

Q1	Commute time (minutes)	Frequency	Midpoint	Midpoint × frequency	[2] (Midpoints – 1 mark) (Midpoint × frequency – 1 mark)
	1 – 10	6	5.5	33	
	11 – 20	16	15.5	248	
	21 – 30	21	25.5	535.5	
	31 – 40	11	35.5	390.5	
	41 – 50	4	45.5	182	
	51 – 60	2	55.5	111	

	$33 + 248 + 535.5 + 390.5 + 182 + 111 = 1500$ **and** $6 + 16 + 21 + 11 + 4 + 2 = 60$	[1]
	$1500 \div 60 = 25$ minutes	[1]
Q2	0.125 **or** $\frac{1}{8}$ oe	[1]
Q3		[4] (Axes labelled correctly and even scale – 1 mark) (All points plotted correctly – 2 marks) (Line of best fit – 1 mark)
	Positive correlation	[1]

Functional Skills Maths Level 2
Revision Fundamentals

Practice Paper Bundle

- ✓ **20** unique functional skills maths level 2 **practice papers** & **mark schemes**
- ✓ **Recommended** by **tutors** and **colleges**
- ✓ **Designed** by **experts**

Revision Cards

- ✓ **Recommended** by **students** and **tutors**
- ✓ Relevant to **all exam boards**
- ✓ Covers **all topics** in your exam

Revision Card and Practice Paper Bundle

- ✓ Papers from the **exam board** of your choice
- ✓ **Explanations**, **practice questions** and **exam questions** on every topic
- ✓ **Save** with the bundle **discount**

Fill your boots...
...with essential **revision supplies**!

Get prepared at pfs.la/shop

Printed in Great Britain
by Amazon